FISH

Created by Gallimard Jeunesse,
Claude Delafosse,
and Sabine Krawczyk
Illustrated by Sabine Krawczyk

A FIRST DISCOVERY BOOK

SCHOLASTIC INC.
New York Toronto London Auckland Sydney

Fish move through water
by using their fins.

Most fish can
only survive
underwater.

Under the scales
is a layer of skin.

Most fish are covered
with scales that protect
their bodies.

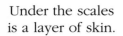

In order for the fish to breathe,
water passes through its gills,
where oxygen is removed.

The skeleton
of the fish
is made of
bones.

To reproduce,
most fish lay eggs.

Watch this
group of fish

run away from
a hungry eel!

Here are some fish from the sea . . .

Sting skate

Cat shark

Sea bream

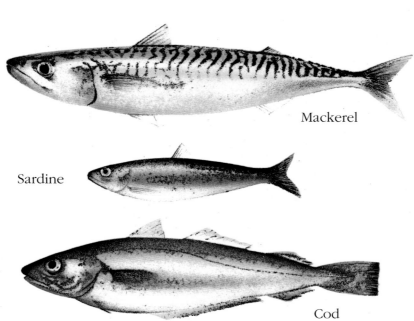

Mackerel

Sardine

Cod

What's hiding
in the sand?

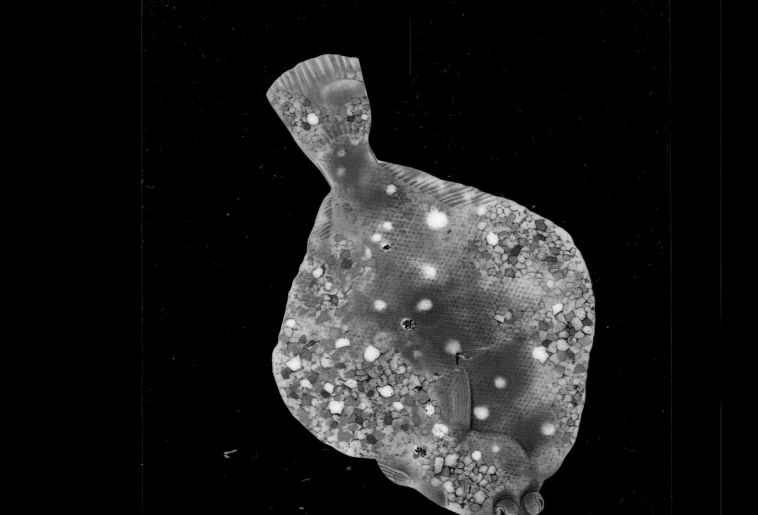

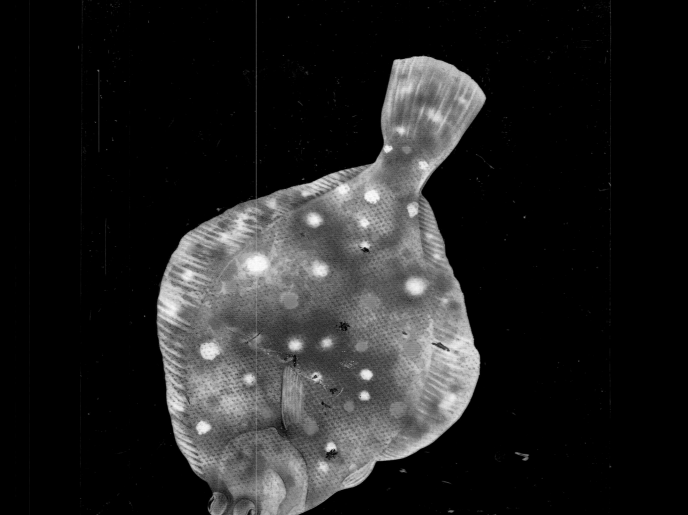

The flounder plays
hide-and-seek by
making itself look
like the ocean
bottom.

What amazing skills!

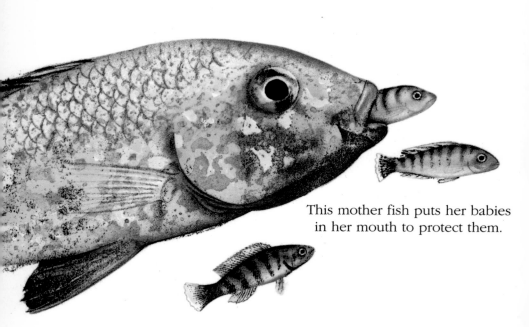

This mother fish puts her babies in her mouth to protect them.

The mother discus
is like a moving restaurant.

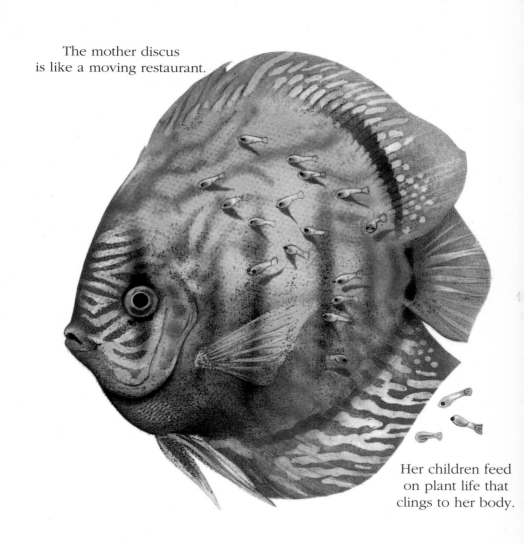

Her children feed
on plant life that
clings to her body.

Because they live in rivers, lakes, and swamps,

Catfish

Minnow

Pike

these are called freshwater fish.

Trout

Bleak

Dace

Shiner

To catch a minnow, you need bait, a fishhook,

A worm attracts
the fish.

Just a bit more
patience . . .

a float, sinkers, and fishing line.

The minnow bites
the worm
and is hooked.

Then pull up
on the fishing line.

This one got away!

What is this little bear
doing in the middle
of the stream?

It's fishing for
salmon that jump
out of the water
while swimming
upstream.

Zebra danio

Gourami

Neon
tetra

Barb

Guppy

Have you ever seen
a freshwater aquarium?

Small catfish

These fish have unusual shapes . . . and wild colors.

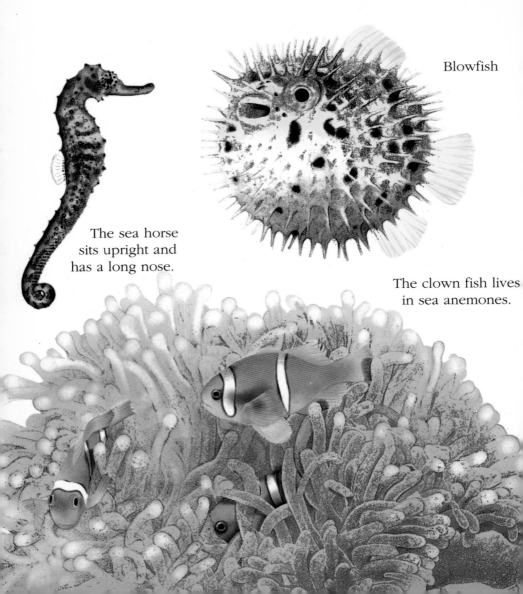

Blowfish

The sea horse sits upright and has a long nose.

The clown fish lives in sea anemones.

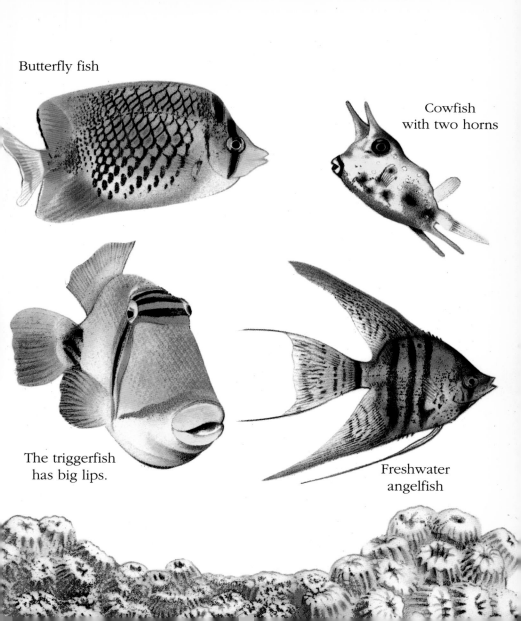

Butterfly fish

Cowfish
with two horns

The triggerfish
has big lips.

Freshwater
angelfish

If you love fish, you can keep a goldfish
as a pet in your home.

Just sprinkle a little food
into the bowl and change
the water once a week.

But some people aren't good at fishing.

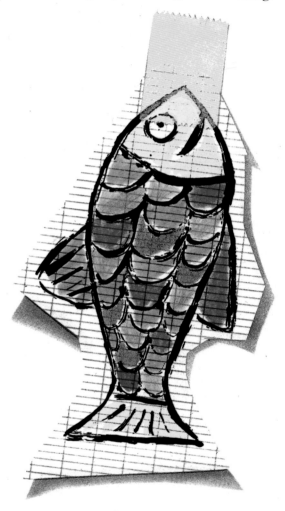

They can only catch fish
they draw themselves.

Parents Magazine
"Best Books" Award

**Parenting Magazine*
Reading Magic Award

****Oppenheim Toy Portfolio*
Gold Seal Award

Library of Congress Cataloging-in-Publication Data available.

Originally published in France under the title *Le poisson* by Editions Gallimard Jeunesse.

ISBN 0-590-38155-5

Copyright © 1994 by Editions Gallimard Jeunesse.
This edition English translation by Heather Miller.
This edition American text by Wendy Barish.
This edition Expert Reader: Karsten Hartel, curatorial associate in Ichthyology, Museum of Comparative Zoology, Harvard University.
All rights reserved. First published in the U.S.A. in 1998 by Scholastic Inc., by arrangement with Editions Gallimard Jeunesse, 5 rue Sebastien-Bottin, F-75007, Paris, France.
SCHOLASTIC and A FIRST DISCOVERY BOOK and associated logos are trademarks and/or registered trademarks of Scholastic Inc.

12 11 10 9 8 7 6 5 4 3 2 1   8 9/9 0 1 2/0

Printed in Italy by Editoriale Libraria
First Scholastic printing, March 1998